—HOW TO PAINT & DRAW—

TECHNIQUES

Written by
Brian Liddle

Intercontinental **Book Productions**

Acknowledgments

The Publishers would like to thank the following for permission to reproduce their photographs: The Tate Gallery, London; pages 59 and 60: The Trustees of the National Gallery; pages 7 (below), 56, 57 (below), 58 and 64 (above and below).
Illustrations by Brian Liddle, except the following: Paul Chapelle; page 41 (above): Samuel Marshall; page 43: Roger Swanborough; pages 28 (right), 29 (above), 32, 33 and 55: John Thompson; pages 50 and 51: Alex Zwarenstein; pages 5, 8, 9, 10, 11 (above), 14, 15, 16, 17, 30, 31 and 53 (below).
Graphic artwork by: Terry Burton, Liz Chapman, and Imperial Artists.

The author gratefully acknowledges textual contributions by Alex Zwarenstein and Roger Swanborough.

Designed and produced by Intercontinental Book Productions Limited, Berkshire House, Queen Street, Maidenhead, Berkshire SL6 1NF.

Copyright ©1981
Intercontinental Book Productions Ltd.

ISBN 0-85047-468-X
Printed in Hong Kong

Contents

Introduction

The wide variety of painting tools, equipment and media available today can create problems for the novice artist. Should he or she begin to draw with charcoal, pencil or ink? Is it best to start painting with watercolor, oil or acrylic paint? What tools are needed for each media? *How to Paint and Draw: Techniques* is designed to provide all the information the beginner needs to know.

The book explores the qualities of a wide variety of media, providing help and interest for both the newcomer and the more advanced amateur painter. In addition to explaining simply and clearly how to use the various materials, step-by-step illustrations guide you through the process of painting various types of subject. Many valuable hints and tips to teach you about methods and media are included, and these will show you how to obtain the special effects used by professional artists to lift their work out of the ordinary.

With this book as a guide, you can quickly learn the basic skills and increase your understanding of the art of painting and drawing. You can then go on to explore the full potential of your materials, learning to use them in ways which will be individual to you.

Why learn techniques?

Every work of art incorporates a degree of technical knowledge and the manipulation of materials to convey a personal message. Technical knowledge may be defined as the ability to carry out the processes which produce the actual work of art. Into this area falls the knowledge necessary to select the materials and prepare the surfaces which will enable the artist to proceed, confident in the knowledge that what he is doing will have the degree of permanence he requires.

In some notable cases the desire to acquire and apply new techniques has led painters to dangerous practices. Perhaps the most famous example was the wide spread use, in Victorian oil paintings, of a bituminous black, used to darken the tone in paintings and achieve the appearance of an Old Master. This not only discolored the oils, but subsequent shrinking during drying caused cracking in many paintings. Most traditional supports are susceptible to temperature and atmospheric variations, and the large departments devoted to the constant repair and renovation of masterpieces in all major galleries testify to the essential impermanence of any painted surface. However, one can ensure by careful method that colors will maintain their density and brightness and that surfaces will not warp and deteriorate at a pace which cannot, with expert care, be reasonably controlled.

Artistic techniques – that is, the methods used to apply the media to the surface – are part and parcel of the artist's uniqueness. Personal techniques should develop out of a search for the means which best serve the individual artist's intentions. However, before arriving at a mature personal statement, which may indeed involve the rejection of orthodox methods, it is usual for the artist to acquire some knowledge of the basic, traditional media and methods. Technical knowledge is evident in any major collection of art, and the student should not only read about and practice his art but also carefully analyze original works of the

Right above and below: *Used as washes, ink is capable of conveying a complete and specific tonal range. Used with a pen it gives an incisiveness no other portable medium can approach. It is unsurpassed as a working medium for re-interpretation as etchings.*

Far right above and below: *Watercolor with its ease of use and sensitivity to the paper surface, wide range of color and glazing capabilities is the ideal medium for sketching but with practice it is capable of major works of art from sketchbook size to large scale.*

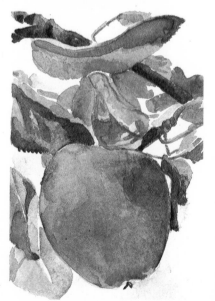

great artists. Oil painting technique was perfected by the Dutch, and they have produced many of the leading artists in this field throughout the centuries. Van Eyck, Rembrandt, Vermeer, and Van Gogh should all be studied. Their personal techniques have been major factors in the development of subsequent generations of artists. In the field of watercolor painting, look at the work of the nineteenth-century English masters, Cotman, Turner, Constable, Cox, and the great American masters of the nineteenth and twentieth centuries, Prendergast, Winslow Homer, Bellows, John Singer Sargent and Hopper. With masterly techniques they were able to achieve, in their chosen media, whatever they desired.

Above: *An example of the kind of brisk, direct brushwork, often painting "wet into wet", that would have been used by Van Gogh.*

Right: The Sunflowers, *perhaps the best known of Van Gogh's motifs, shows his painting technique at its peak. Van Gogh spoke of the flowers fading quickly and having to do the "whole thing in one rush". It is unlikely that Van Gogh found it necessary to draw in the whole motif first with charcoal; the drawing and coloring are of the "alla prima" or first time method. Repainting is superfluous.*

Lead pencil

Pencil is one of the most flexible mediums that the artist has at his disposal. It is easily transportable without being messy, can be erased, can be incisive and hard, or soft and sympathetic, and, in conjunction with a sketch pad or other suitable surface, can always be on hand for drawing and sketching.

The subject matter will often suggest the type of pencil to be used; a soft, misty landscape may dictate the use of a soft pencil, used on its side to make a

Left and below: *Subtle crosshatch using HB and F pencils.*

Above: *A brisk broken treatment completes the modeling of the figure, again working with two grades.*

soft, diffuse mark, while the characterization of an old man's face may suggest a linear rendering with a harder grade of pencil. With this in mind, build up a collection of lead or graphite pencils from the very softest at 8B to the hardest at 9H. At the soft end of the range of graphite pencils, a 6B gives a very soft, fluid line when the point is used and a flat tonal area when the side of the point is used.

The middle range, HB, B, and 2B, are useful for a drawing that you wish to sustain over a long period – a day's landscape drawing or a life class of several hours duration. Start off with a

very light underdrawing, gradually building up the tone with the B and 2B pencils when you are confident that the proportions are correct. A 2H pencil is useful for light underdrawing. These pencils should be kept sharp because their prime characteristic is incisiveness. Also, a pencil that most draughtsmen find indispensable is the F grade, which strikes a balance between hardness and softness, and is the ideal sketching pencil.

Carbon and other pencils

Compared to the common lead or graphite pencil, carbon pencils, available in grades of hard to soft, give a blacker, chalkier

The studies on this page show the different effects and moods which can be achieved using medium to soft grades of pencil. Underneath each main picture is a detail showing the actual pencil strength. Moving left to right from the top the grades used are: F, HB, B, 3B and 5B.

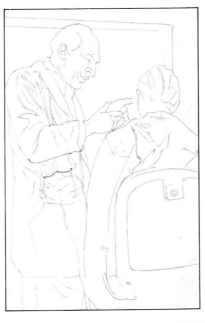

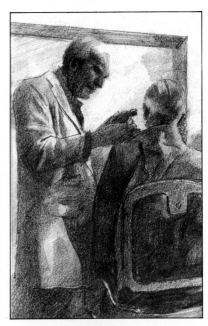

line which can be diffused with an eraser or paper stump. There are also the black conté pencils in three grades: No.1 (medium) No.2 (soft), and No.3 (extra soft), which give a very interesting quality of mark, a little greasier than carbon, not quite as easily diffused, but capable of great depth; a line can be gone over several times, becoming richer and darker in quality. Another plus for the conté pencil and its equivalent conté crayon is that they come in harmonious earth colors — red sanguine, sepia, and bistre, as well as white.

There are many other types of pencil available, including clutch pencils, graphite sticks, and mechanical pencils and holders, which are worth experimenting with for their different qualities of mark and handling.

Above: *Very sharp F and HB pencils were used lightly to convey the essential qualities of a ballerina. Erasing should be avoided in a drawing of this nature, which depends on delicacy of line.*

Above: *Using pencil grades from H to 3B, subtle modulations of tone are achieved in this study by predominant use of continuous shading using the side of the point, rather than crosshatching.*

Charcoal

Charcoal, in the traditional form of willow or vine charcoal sticks, is the oldest drawing medium, and, for the beginner, is most successfully employed for larger drawings. Whereas the pencil mark can be very tightly controlled, a large charcoal drawing demands broader treatment. The special quality of charcoal is its ability to cover large areas quickly and to be erased by simply dusting off the page. It is a wonderful medium for inspiring drawing confidence because of its flexibility and unfussiness, and these qualities should be enjoyed. For detailed drawing, a hard grade charcoal pencil will give the best results.

Paper and tools

A sharpener, heavy-handled cutting knife, or craft knife

Left: *An unsharpened B pencil was used very lightly to give a soft edge effect. Although "unfinished", no further work is required for a satisfactory picture.*

Above: *A complete contrast of mood is seen in this picture, where vigorous use is made of 4B and 6B pencils. A hard surface paper was chosen to maintain the heavy black qualities of the lead.*

Above: *F and B pencils were used in this drawing, which contains many subtle and difficult passages. The pencils were kept very sharp, shading essentially by the continuous tone technique.*

Above: *The motif suggested the use of conté crayons with their range of earth-colored tones. Conté crayons can be sharpened to a point, but cannot be used over or together with lead pencil.*

should be to hand to keep pencils in optimum working condition. An eraser is also important, not only for erasing mistakes, but also for blending and lifting out lines using the edge or point. There are several types of eraser available; natural, gum, plastic, and kneaded. The natural erasers come in grades of softness, the harder ones being useful for taking out deeply incised lines, the softer for softer lines and charcoal. A kneaded eraser is also useful and can be shaped to suit requirements.

Other erasers should be kept clean by rubbing them on a clean piece of paper, to avoid spoiling the drawing.

The mark the pencil makes will be affected by the grain of the paper and the hardness of its surface. A hard pencil, (any of the H range) will work best on a fine-grained paper. A soft, dark pencil, although quite suitable

Left: *Using a middle grade of black conté pencil a rich tonal effect can be achieved as well as the necessary sharpness in defining the features.*

for a fine-grained paper, is very effective on a rougher grain, giving a textured quality. Scale will, of course, determine the grade of pencil used; a small technical drawing will require a hard pencil and therefore a fine-grained paper.

Colored papers can extend the range of possible effects. Do not choose a dark tone of paper, unless you intend to use white for the highlights, or the drawing will lose its impact.

Drawing by use of point-relationship

Though some basic understanding of the laws of perspective are helpful to the artist, conveying a three-dimensional scene onto a two-dimensional surface can be achieved quite successfully by drawing using the point-relationship method. The shape and size of the paper or canvas must be able to contain the motif. For example, in

this drawing it was quickly apparent that the motif could be contained in a square and that the boat was tilted slightly to the right. First, draw a vertical line down through the center of the paper or canvas. This should correspond with the center of

The four drawings of a boat on these pages demonstrate an easy way of building up a picture accurately without a formal knowledge of perspective.

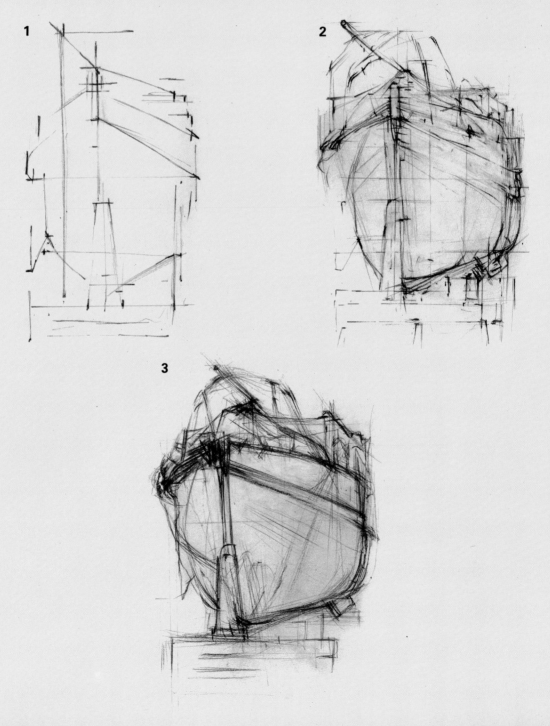

1

2

3

the motif and is also the center of vision. Holding the pencil at arm's length, use it to measure across the motif to determine how many lengths of the pencil are needed to define the extremities of the subject. Working either side of the center line, and also along the center line itself, you will be able to establish the top and bottom limits of the drawing.

When these points have been fixed, use the pencil to deter-mine the angles of the main features. Move across the motif in all directions, measuring distances and relative sizes. A spider's web of marks fixing internal features and sub-divisions will result. Although the objects in front of you may be foreshortened, distances, heights, and recessional depths can be determined and fixed with confidence.

As you include in the drawing the finer details of the subject, the web of lines used to plot the drawing can either be erased or, preferably, absorbed into the drawing. Begin to convey volume by shading in the mass areas.

Should the drawing be the basis for a painting, a brush should be used at this point to block in the main masses and tonal areas. First, however, you should rub down or dust off the pencil or charcoal so that it will not dirty the paint.

4

Colored pencil

Colored pencils have come into their own as a serious artistic medium due to the advent of the new, less inhibited styles of the Pop artists. The informality of colored pencil, previously regarded as a pleasant and straightforward marker for children, is capable of a very wide range of applications in the hands of an expert.

A tremendous range of colors is available. These can be overlaid in a glaze technique and can also be laid flat to give bright, opaque areas. The blending possibilities have been exploited by commercial illustrators to a breathtaking degree of photo-realism, while the humorous, elegant, and decorative drawings of David Hockney illustrate a very different approach.

There are also several brands of water-soluble pencils. As the name implies, these can be turned into a watercolor medium, either by dipping the pencil in water as one works or by first completing the work and then brushing water over it to blend the colors. The pencils are available in packs and are also sold separately so suitable colors can be selected. A full range of greens from one manufacturer may have two or three gaps which can be filled by greens

1

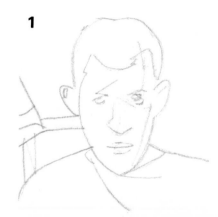

2

3

Above: *A wide range of pencil colors is available.*

Left: *In the first drawing, a light blue was used to determine the larger shapes of the figure. In the second, a fine coloring determined the predominant local color of each area. In the third stage, overlays of warm colors built up the flesh tones while cool colors were used in the shadows.*

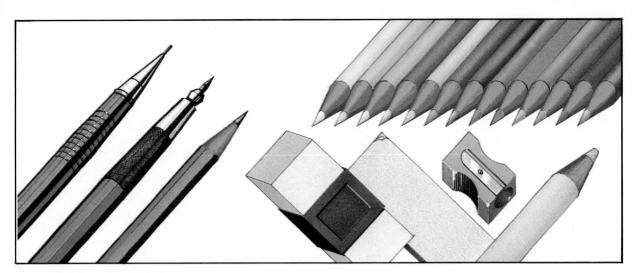

from another manufacturer.

Many types of paper are suitable for colored pencils but a smooth white drawing paper is perhaps the best. The paper should not be too highly glazed,

Above: *A range of mechanical lead pencils and the most-used colored pencils, together with various tools for erasing and sharpening.*

Right: *Detail in the face is carefully worked up, preserving it as the focus of interest while the rest is allowed to disintegrate.*

Below: *Do not be afraid to work without preliminary drawing, altering the forms until correct.*

so that the pencil mark will not skid. A hard, white paper will give brilliance, grained papers texture, and colored papers are best for "mood" drawings. Dark, subdued papers can be very effective, giving an added brilliance to the colors.

To remove mistakes, clean, hard plastic erasers are best. Use a typist's eraser as the last resort as it will roughen the paper and make subsequent blending impossible. For very localized corrections, an eraser shield will prove very useful.

Making your mark

The scale of the work is an important consideration; do not attempt anything too big as the quality of the mark may lack interest and appear very mechanical. The incisiveness and range of the pencil is best exploited on a small, intimate scale. Keep in mind the capacity of the pencils for overglazing and for hatching one color over another allowing the color beneath to show through.

To lay a large, flat area smoothly is one of the most difficult techniques, as the slightest variation in pressure will introduce a change of tone. This is best done using a long, well-blunted point to the pencil. To obtain a dark, even area build up the color in several flat layers. Laying light colors over dark is possible, but heavy pressure is needed and control is difficult in small areas. A crisp, hard edge to

Above: *The first stage of this landscape concerned the drawing of the composition, when a light tint of color was given to each area. In the second stage, detail was applied by overlaying colors – "glazing" – until the desired tone and modeling was achieved.*

Right: *To convey the effect of sunlight on the patterned deck chairs, the composition was carefully considered and strong colors were built up solidly alongside one another and very rarely glazed, except where the range of color needed to be extended.*

an area of color is easily achieved by covering the edge of the area with a strip of thin paper and shading over onto it.

With the wide range of hues available, and the many variations of tone, one can build up subtle gradations in color, or create abrupt changes in tone and color, resulting in a very lively picture. A lesson in how to do this successfully can be learned by rendering a favorite painting in colored pencil, trying to match the tones and colors.

Portraits and landscapes

For portrait sketches include flesh color, pink, crimson, red, cobalt blue, cadmium yellow, dark blue, and purple. Begin by sketching in the proportions of the face; this underdrawing will finally disappear under the warm flesh tones if the intitial drawing is kept light. Color the area of the face with the flesh-colored pencil and add modeling with the red, yellow, and blue. Remember that cool colors, such

as blues, greens, and purples, are often found in shadows, while warm colors, such as reds and yellows, are found in lighted areas.

In landscape sketching, use predominantly blues and greens, plus two types of red and cadmium yellow. Draw out the proportions as before and cover the whole area lightly with what you see as the predominant colors in the scene. This is then gradually modified by working with the other colors.

Pastels

Pastels are pure pigment held together with the minimum of binding material. Fine, soft pastels are made by British, French, Dutch, and American firms.

They are graded and priced according to the pigment used.

Blending pastels

Although the colors can certainly be blended, not more than three colors can be mixed together before the brilliance of the color goes. This means that artists working in pastels tend to extend their number of colors so that undue blending is unnecessary. Fortunately, there is an immense range of beautiful colors available.

There are two methods of blending. One is physical, actually welding colors together on the paper, the other is optical, when the blending is done by the eye as it reads colors in close proximity.

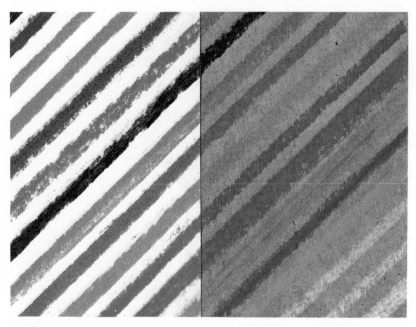

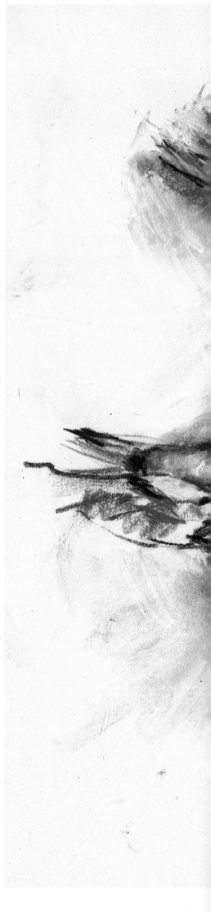

Above: *A selection of pastels, drawn across two tones of paper, demonstrating how a color is modified by the background color. As is apparent, pastel cannot be easily applied in a tidy and mechanical fashion.*

Right: *Blending can be achieved by a moderate amount of rubbing or smoothing together of colors, or, in a more sophisticated way, allowing strokes of colors on different layers to break through, forming optical blending.*

Opposite: *This drawing uses both techniques; blending is evident in the area of shadow under the heads of the fishes while the sheen of the scales is conveyed by the use of broken flecks of color. The eyes and wrapping paper are straight application of color.*

Surfaces

It is helpful to begin using pastels on a toned surface, such as Gray Bogus paper. Brown wrapping paper and construction paper are also useful.

A close look at many of Lautrec's pastels reveals the brilliant incorporation of the background color into the picture. Although, as with watercolors, drawing with pastels on a rough-surfaced paper gives a brilliance to the medium, it is extremely extravagant of materials, acting on the pastels almost like a grater on cheese. The pace of the drawing on very rough papers is slowed down by the sheer effort of building up enough pigment to give density.

First attempts

The medium demands certain sympathetic and intelligently selected motifs to bring out its best characteristics; speed, beautiful color, and texture.

Degas, another master of pastel, is well worth close study. His method was to build up form in a series of layers, each one fixed, using immensely confident and informed strokes to convey tone, texture, light, and form. The genius of Degas and Lautrec lay in their ability to retain the bigness of the medium and yet convey the most subtle and intimate detail. Begin with a motif which lends itself to simplification. This does not mean that the motif cannot be trees, flowers, etc; but try to convey mass in your first efforts. The medium should not be used like a thick pencil. Motifs which contain lettering, fine detail such as small patterns on clothing, linear detail, and small natural form should be either avoided when selecting a subject, or ignored or simplified when working on the motif.

Although your first attempts will probably be crude, with experience you will learn when to rub or blend together, when to exploit the effect of separate strokes, when to leave a solid color area and where a flick of color could be placed most

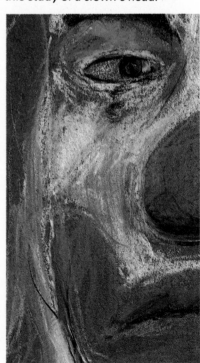

Othello crayons, although not as solid in body color as traditional pastels, can be sharpened and used to convey quite fine detail, as seen in this study of a clown's head.

effectively. When the drawing is complete, decide whether to fix the pastel or not. Fixing, while stabilizing the powder, also acts as a coagulant and sometimes stains. By applying fixative too heavily, the tones of the work can be changed instantly and irrevocably and spots of fixative which will not evaporate will be clearly visible. The lightest of deposits, applied with a mouth diffuser, rather than an aerosol, is recommended. Apply three coats at ten-minute intervals. Alternatively, protect the work with tissue and frame.

Inevitably, pastels break into smaller and smaller pieces in use, the paper sleeves no longer protect them, and they offset on one another. The contents of a box can become a collection of mud-colored fragments. A stroke on the side of the paper reveals the former brilliance, but only periodic cleaning with a soft cloth or keeping similar hues together in separate boxes can overcome this.

Pastel need not be a painstaking medium to use. This figure study captures the essentials of the model while retaining a bigness and directness in the drawing.

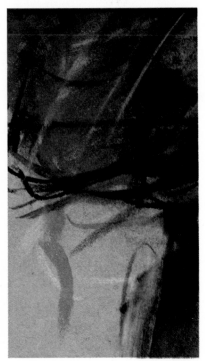

Pen and ink

The most widely used drawing ink is waterproof black, traditionally called India ink. It is excellent for reproduction and allows mistakes to be whited out. It also tolerates fluids which may inadvertently be spilled on it. Its main drawbacks are a tendency to become less viscose as the bottle is increasingly exposed to air, and terrific staining power – it is practically impossible to remove from clothes or paper.

A wide variety of brands is available, from American, British, and German manufacturers. Each brand has a slightly different viscosity and denseness. Experiment with several to find out which one suits your particular way of drawing. Use non-waterproof ink if you wish to reactivate the line

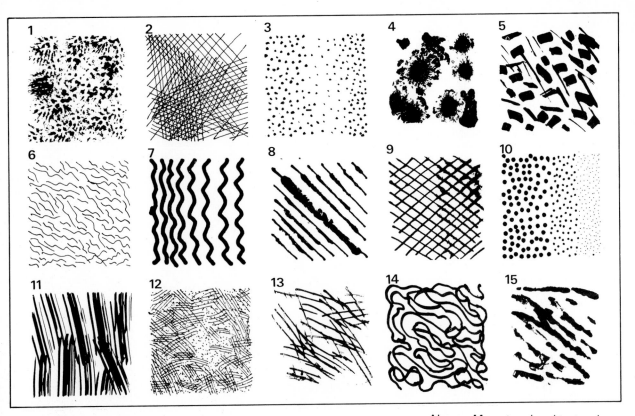

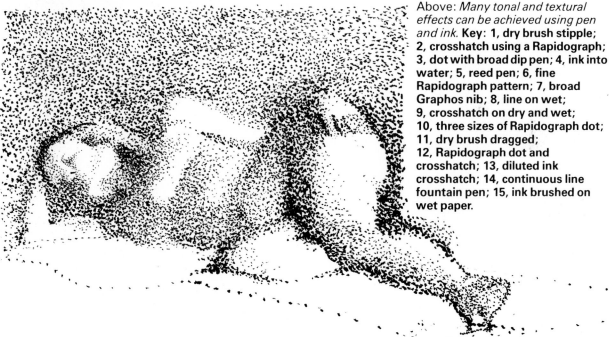

Above: *Many tonal and textural effects can be achieved using pen and ink.* **Key: 1, dry brush stipple; 2, crosshatch using a Rapidograph; 3, dot with broad dip pen; 4, ink into water; 5, reed pen; 6, fine Rapidograph pattern; 7, broad Graphos nib; 8, line on wet; 9, crosshatch on dry and wet; 10, three sizes of Rapidograph dot; 11, dry brush dragged; 12, Rapidograph dot and crosshatch; 13, diluted ink crosshatch; 14, continuous line fountain pen; 15, ink brushed on wet paper.**

Opposite above: *There is a very wide range of pens available to the artist, from the finest steel nibs to calligraphic nibs.*

Left: *Using a fountain pen, this river boat scene was completed in a short period of sustained drawing, without any initial pencil work.*

Above: *The use of the dot technique in pen drawing is slow – tone must be carefully observed and the distribution of the dots controlled to convey contour, form and tone. An initial pencil underdrawing will help when assessing the correct distribution of the dots, which should be built up gradually.*

A straightforward sketch using a dip pen. Tone has been conveyed by crosshatching but the drawing retains an open quality.

for tonal and decorative effect. A range of colored inks is also available. The colors tend to be harsh, but all inks can be diluted and modified with purified water, which is recommended because it is free from basic impurities present in local water supplies and the colors retain their freshness.

Tools and surfaces

Practically any smooth, non-greasy surface – paper, board, or acetate – is suitable for drawing on. The surface need not be impervious or hard, and there is usually no need to stretch the paper.

Any tool that will convey the ink can be used, depending upon your patience and curiosity. Pens and brushes are the most popular tools. Do not habitually use your best sable brushes for ink, as drawing ink will eventually destroy their whip. Brushes must be thoroughly cleaned in soapy water immediately after use, working the soap well in toward the ferrule to remove all traces of ink.

Dip pens
These are the most simple and direct of pens. A wide range of inexpensive steel nibs and holders are available. Remove the slight greasiness from a new nib by quickly passing it through a gentle flame (prolonged heat will ruin the temper of the nib). It takes some hours of drawing to break in a new nib. A slight build-up of ink on the nib is quite acceptable, though too much will impair its flexibility. Nibs can be scraped clean with a knife, though this may roughen and damage them – time for a new one.

Quill and reed pens have sensitivity and pliability, and were used by masters like Rembrandt

and Van Gogh. Reed pens are still available but quill pens, which require lengthy and highly skilled preparation, are now very rare.

Reservoir pens
Popular and relatively new pens for ink drawing are the Rapidograph and its variants. These tools are designed for engineering and architectural drawing use, and give a continuous flow of ink due to a generous reservoir and specially designed valve system. A variety of expensive monoline nibs, ranging from 0.1mm to 2mm in width, are obtainable. The uniform line they give can be used effectively, though their inflexibility does impose a decorative bias on the drawing. The nibs always remain hard and mechanical in feeling. A

special range of inks, black and some colors, is used.

Ancillary materials

Useful extras when working in pen and ink include blotting paper, rags, and porcelain mixing palettes. Ink stains are almost indelible so do not use your watercolor box lid to hold ink. Keep a spare bottle or two of ink handy.

Drawing on site

Confidence is essential when drawing on site with pen and ink. Nervousness and impatience are transmitted very obviously when working in a medium as unequivocal as black line. Drawing out the motif carefully with a pencil as a guide

Drawing directly with a medium size oil painting brush results in a powerful and decorative study.

should be dispensed with as soon as possible, as it leads to lifeless drawing and will stifle the enjoyment which increases as your confidence grows.

Pen technique can consist of short staccato strokes, mainly in one direction, to build up the form, or be used in a very open technique. When drawing subjects which move, continue drawing despite the inevitable inaccuracies which occur. A degree of exitement will be conveyed if you remain with the motif and keep drawing.

One small factor which can prove a major irritant is the level of ink in the bottle dropping to a point where the nib constantly needs replenishing. Keep the bottle topped up. Buy a large bottle and fill your small bottles before the day's outing. While a medium deposit of ink will dry on the paper quite rapidly, very heavy deposits can take several hours to dry out completely because of the lacquer content.

Working with colored inks

The brilliance of colored ink is enhanced by using a good-quality white, smooth paper or even one of the lighter-weight watercolor papers. The paper should be stretched if you intend using wash. Inks can be used in

exactly the same way as watercolors. Purified water is recommended for easy flow and to lessen a tendency to streakiness. However, any wash which is allowed to dry before completion will leave a hard edge, as ink cannot be reactivated like watercolor. Underpainting in bright colors is very difficult to subdue as subsequent layers of color tend to give a dirty or very crude effect.

Use as few colors as possible when sketching with inks to avoid a tendency to garishness. Here, three colors and black were used.

Oil painting

Oil paints have a quality and flexibility of handling which, when well used, cannot be rivaled by any other medium, even the recently developed acrylic paints.

Painting mediums

Oil paint consists of dry pigment powder held in suspension by a drying vegetable oil that acts as a binder. A painting medium is used to make the paint easier to apply and also to thin down its consistency.

Many ready-made mediums are available, each having its own use and application. The most common is a mixture of linseed oil and turpentine, but it does have the disadvantage of being slow-drying. Mediums that contain varnish, stand oil, or beeswax overcome this problem and will help to prevent the paint dripping when heavily thinned. Driers are available to shorten the drying time, but they should be used with care as too high a proportion will impair the paint surface.

When choosing mediums, consider the finish required: for a shiny finish, use a varnish medium, and for a matt finish one that contains beeswax.

Diluents or solvents like turpentine and mineral spirits, which are used for cleaning brushes and palettes, can also be mixed with mediums for further thinning. When used on their own, the binding power of the oil paint is impaired, and the paint surface is liable to crack.

Brushes

It is important to have a good selection of hog hair and sable brushes. Sable brushes give a smoother, softer stroke than hog hair and are usually kept for fine work and detail. Various synthetic brushes are also available.

Most brushes come in a variety of shapes: bright, flat, round, and filbert. Brights have short bristles, and are used for applying thick, creamy paint. Flats are useful for broad and direct work, rounds for small areas and for applying heavily thinned paint. Filberts make shaped, tapering marks.

All come in a range of sizes, usually from 1 (the smallest) up to 12, but larger sizes are available. A good working selection of brushes would include several sizes of each of the basic shapes.

Right: *Stretching and priming a canvas; stretcher pieces are slotted together to form a rectangle of the proportions required. Check the corners are square by measuring the diagonals. Fold the canvas round the sides of the stretchers and using a staple gun, secure the canvas to the center of the outside edges. Repeat on the other two sides, stapling at 2-inch intervals, to within a few inches of the corners. Fold and staple the corners.*

There are many methods of preparing absorbent surfaces to receive oil paints. A traditional method is to apply three coats of size to the surface – following the manufacturer's instructions – and follow by two coats of white canvas primer, allowing twenty four hours drying time between each coat.

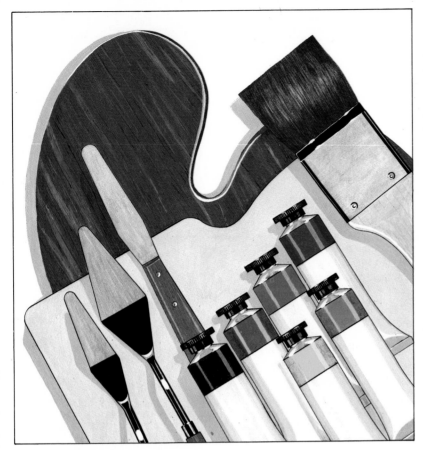

Brushes should be carefully looked after, removing paint with mineral spirits or turpentine, and then washing them with soap and water. Do not leave brushes standing in solvent for any length of time.

Palettes and other tools

Palette knives are useful for mixing paints and cleaning the palette, and can also be used as painting knives for applying thick paint directly to the canvas.

A shaped, wooden palette is useful, but any non-absorbent surface such as glass or plastic will do the job.

Palette cups – small open cans for holding oil and turpentine – are convenient, as they can be clipped to hand-held palettes, but any suitable container can be used.

A large range of easels is available, from large, studio ones to the small sketching variety. The choice will depend on your requirements.

Surfaces

The most widely used painting surface or support for oil paint is canvas. This material is ideal when stretched and primed with a suitable ground. Wood, ply-

Opposite: *Try a wide variety of shapes and sizes of brush before you decide on the particular shape or quality of brush which suits you best. It is a mistake to try to economise by using only two or three.*

Above: *The traditional wood palette has a useful mid-tone to help evaluate the colors. A varnishing brush should be large, and painting knives with their delicate temper are necessary for applying paint in the more detailed passages.*

wood, metal, cardboard, and paper are alternatives, but require careful preparation.

The simplest but most expensive way of obtaining a canvas is to buy one ready stretched and primed. Commercially prepared boards which have a simulated canvas surface are also available. Many artists prefer to prepare their own supports, buying the linen, cotton, and hessian canvas and stretching and priming it themselves. Linen is the best support, but a good quality cotton is almost as good. Hessian is very coarse and requires a lot of priming. The shiny surface of hardboard provides an alternative to canvas, but it must be battened and sized to prevent warping.

Both oil- and acrylic-based primers are available for use with oil paints. The support must be given a coat of glue size solution before an oil-based primer is used. The primer should be applied in two thin coats, as one thick coat may crack and leave an uneven, shiny surface.

Using oil paints

Oil paint is a highly flexible medium and, while all painters develop their own approach to it, some understanding of its basic uses and capabilities is important when starting.

Right: *Three ways of applying oil paint: from top to bottom;* scumbling *is opaque paint applied over another layer in an irregular way;* glazes *are created by laying thin coats of paint, diluted with a suitable medium, over a painted surface;* stippling *is useful for producing broken areas of color. Apply the paint in dots or short strokes.*

The one rule for oils is to use "fat over lean", which means that the oil content of the medium is increased with each layer of paint. This will stop the surface cracking as the paint begins to dry.

Oils can be used for carefully planned works that are built up layer by layer, or in a very direct and spontaneous manner, often using thick, impasto paint to express the immediacy and feel of a subject. Impasto is paint mixed with a resinous medium or gel, and applied with a brush or knife. This creates a surface texture, and the expressive quality of the brush strokes can be used to build up form and movement within a composition.

Painting "wet into wet" is the technique of applying a color on top of another that is still wet so that the colors blend or run into each other. This technique is particularly useful in very direct and immediate forms of painting.

Some surfaces suitable for oil painting are, left to right; Daler board, primed hardboard, canvas-surfaced board, linen canvas.

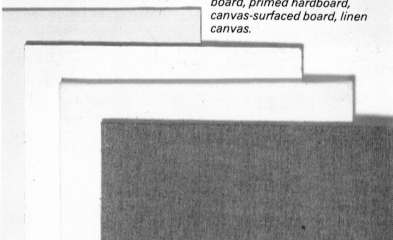

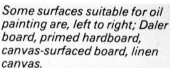

Above: *While oil paint comes in a wide range of colors, a limited palette can be used to good effect as can be seen in this still-life. The colors used were; titanium white, French ultramarine, sap green, cadmium yellow, yellow ochre, vermillion and alizarin crimson.*

Right: *Color is a very personal matter, but a useful palette for the beginner would include (reading clockwise); titanium white, lemon yellow, yellow ochre, cadmium red, light red, rose madder, burnt umber, burnt sienna, cobalt blue and French ultramarine. Greens, like oranges and purples, are not essential as they can be mixed, though viridian green and terre verte are particularly useful.*

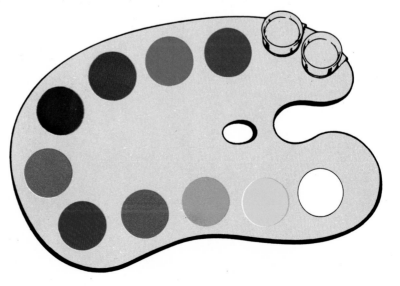

Enlarging drawings

A drawing can be simply transferred to another surface by tracing the original should no enlargement be required. If, however, you want to enlarge a detail of your drawing or scale up the drawing as a whole, you can use one of two methods.

Method 1

Mark out points at equal intervals along all four sides of the drawing or the detail you wish to enlarge. Do the same, but to a larger scale, along the four sides of the canvas or surface onto which the image is to be transferred. Join these points with straight lines from one side of the drawing to the other thus creating a series of squares. Using this grid as a guide, copy each section of the drawing in large-scale.

Method 2

Draw diagonal lines from corner to corner of the drawing. Then draw vertical and horizontal lines through the center point out to the four sides. This will create a "quartering" of the drawing which can be subdivided again and again until an appropriate grid is created.

Portrait painting

Begin by roughing out the proportions of the portrait in pencil or a light, neutral color — make no attempt to draw detail because this will inhibit the initial blocking in of the tone (figure 1).

Having done this, mix a basic flesh tone on your palette and apply it to cover the whole area of the face (figure 2). There are many formulae which can be used when mixing a basic flesh tone. Examples include a mixture of venetian red, yellow ochre and white, or a mixture of alizarin crimson, yellow ochre, and white, with a touch of cobalt blue (the latter will provide a pinker flesh tone).

Lay in the basic color of the

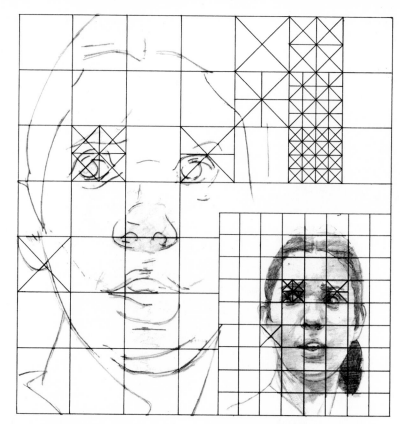

background and clothing; it need be only a diluted application to achieve a quick initial coverage (figure 3). You can now draw further detail into the portrait with a very fine pointed brush (figure 4).

Modify local color by adding to the flesh tone on the palette some of the colors that you laid around your palette. On the parts that are in shadow, you will want the flesh tone to be a little cooler, so add some cobalt blue; for a warmer touch add an appropriate red, and so on (figure

5). At this stage rely on your powers of observation and not on formulae. You will find that by looking at the sitter and seeing the color as a cool or warm tone you will be able to mix an equivalent on your palette.

Still-life painting

In oil painting the still-life is one of the most commonly used themes. It can be as simple or complex as the artist wishes and, being an indoor subject,

can be kept in a constant position and light. It can be used to explore problems in isolation or in combination with others. Two major considerations are depth and form, but contrast of shape, color, and texture can be equally exploited.

Composing a still-life

A still life can either be a formal, conscious arrangement or an existing "found" group of objects. The most obvious method is to arrange selected

5

items on a surface until a satisfactory pictorial arrangement is achieved.

However, it is very easy to create a series of stilted and lifeless subjects. Always include contrasts in shape, in scale, both horizontal and vertical, and in color and texture. Look at the still-life from different angles and eye levels to find the most interesting viewpoint. Take careful note of the background as it is as much a part of the composition as the objects themselves. Try to visualize exactly how the arrangement will fit the canvas. As an aid, cut a small rectangle of the same proportions as the canvas from a sheet of paper and use it as a viewfinder. It is worthwhile making a number of quick sketches of the basic shapes, masses, and proportions to see how the group works as a two-dimensional composition.

Step-by-step painting

Once you are satisfied with the arrangement, it can be drawn on the canvas in charcoal, pencil, or thinned paint (figure 1). The basic shapes and tones are then laid (figure 2), using a large brush and thinned paint. Neutral colors are often used for this underpainting, as the tonal considerations are more important at this stage. After the initial broad underpainting, shapes, form, and color are more clearly defined (figure 3) and the drawing reworked and adjusted. In the final stage (figure 4), details are added with a fine brush. Always work from the general to the particular. The whole surface should be covered before thinking about specific details.

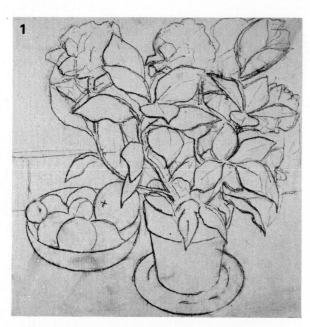

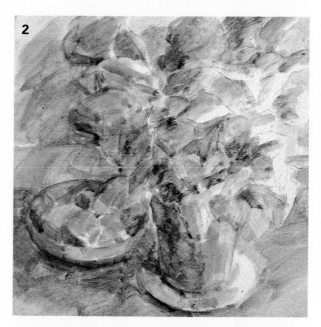

Right: *When painting with a palette knife, use the pigment direct from the tube, with little or no medium. Do not be afraid to apply the paint liberally.*

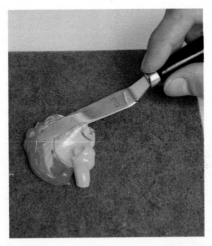

Below: *Painting with a palette knife is a direct and forceful technique. Keep the motifs in initial exercises simple. Color is laid on broadly and worked into while still wet. The marks and texture of the paint will play an important role in the picture. Several palette and painting knives can be used in one picture to give a variety of effects.*

Sketching in oils

It is important when working outside to have all your equipment well organized. A lightweight, collapsable sketching easel and a stool are important pieces of equipment, especially when working in places where a good deal of carrying and traveling are involved.

Always check that you have everything you need before setting out, and make sure that there is sufficient paint in the tubes for the work that is planned.

Mediums and solvents should be in leakproof containers and the palette should be light and easy to hold.

Sketching technique

The aim of sketching in oils should be to capture the essence of a particular scene or mo-ment. When making landscape sketches, a direct or alla prima method of painting is usually employed. With this approach a painting is completed in a single session, using opaque colors. The paint is applied freely with a brush or knife capturing the freshness of color and feeling of a place.

It requires confidence because the artist must work quickly and boldly and must not be afraid to change passages in the picture either by overpainting or scraping off.

Sketches can be used as working drawings for studio paintings, but these often lack the life and vitality of the initial statement.

In the sketch above, the paint was applied with no underpainting or drawing. Areas of color were applied directly, the dark colors and tones being put down first, and worked into while still

Above: *This picture contains many of the elements normally encountered on a day's landscape sketching. A selection of sable brushes – none larger than size 8 – was used, because of the fine detail of the foliage and the distances.*

Opposite: *The first stage shows a quick but thorough record of the main elements of the scene. Speed was necessary as storm clouds threatened rain. The oil content was kept low to speed drying. As the work progressed, the trees on the right were removed, allowing a more dramatic rendering of the wooden gates against the sky.*

wet. Mistakes can be wiped or scraped out.

The painting of lock gates on the facing page (top) was stopped after one hour. In the next stage this initial statement has been worked up and refined, although all the important elements were already established.

Acrylics

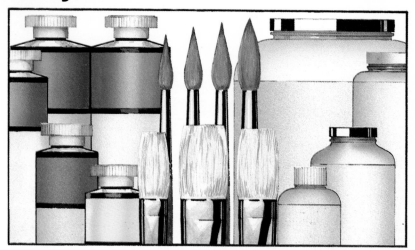

Acrylics are a recent innovation developed originally for large, exterior murals. They are extremely flexible and can be used in a variety of ways. Made from pigment bound in a synthetic resin, the paint can be thinned with water and dries to form a waterproof layer. Speed in drying makes acrylic a very convenient medium.

The color range is similar to oils, but some of the names are different because new synthetic dyes and pigments have been developed.

They can be applied to virtually any dry, oil-free surface. Canvas can be used unprimed, or with a ground of acrylic primer. Brushes and equipment are the same as for oils. Brushes should be thoroughly cleaned with soap and water immediately after use to prevent hardening.

Acrylic mediums

The mediums for use with acrylics are cloudy or milky in the bottle, becoming transparent when dry. The combination of mediums and acrylics can produce many interesting effects.

There are gloss and matt mediums for both general painting and glazing and a gel medium for impasto work. A thick modeling paste is also

Above: *A range of the most useful brush sizes and types of acrylics available.*

Right: *Two beach cabins made an ideal subject for acrylics. The sand in the foreground and at the side of the cabins was rendered using a dry brush and small quantities of paint, dragged across the surface. Details of the weathered woodwork were added using the smallest sizes of brushes.*

available. For very thick impasto, gel or modeling paste is mixed with a small amount of color. Paints can be used with water alone in a similar technique to that employed for watercolors. However, the addition of at least a drop of

Left: *Acrylics can be applied in many ways. From left to right: very dilute "watercolor" wash technique; impasto using a palette knife; impasto using a brush; glazing over impasto using a diluted top coat.*

medium will help the paint to flow more easily, and will give greater depth and body to washes. An acrylic retarder can be used to slow the drying time and painting "wet into wet" is made easier by its use.

Using acrylic paint

While acrylics are frequently employed using a watercolor technique and the traditional oil-painting techniques of building up a picture by underpainting and overglazing, they do lend themselves naturally to a direct approach.

However, before starting to paint with acrylics, a certain amount of planning is necessary. It is important to consider the effects you wish to achieve. These can range from the illustrative considerations of the subject matter (what it is, and what is happening) to the impressionistic and expressive qualities of light and color, movement and feeling.

While it is important to be flexible and keep an open mind on the subject so that new ideas can be seen and exploited as the work progresses, remember that acrylics do not allow quite the same scope as oils. Unlike oils, which can still be moved about, scraped, or wiped off some time after application, acrylics leave little time for deliberation or change once they have been laid down. Brush marks dry precisely as they are made, and the tactile or surface quality of the paint should be considered in the overall plan of the composition.

1

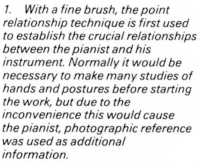

1. With a fine brush, the point relationship technique is first used to establish the crucial relationships between the pianist and his instrument. Normally it would be necessary to make many studies of hands and postures before starting the work, but due to the inconvenience this would cause the pianist, photographic reference was used as additional information.
2. Basic local color is applied in a "watercolor" technique using medium size brushes.
3. The general tonal areas of the subject become more defined and structural and specific details of the stool and piano are added. The paint is used more heavily to convey solidity and mass in the main elements.
4. In the final stage, the tones and colors are adjusted and the positions of the hands and feet are thoroughly worked out. Some of the original watercolor effect is retained as being adequate to explain the qualities of the wood and some shadow areas. For the more crucial areas of the hands and face, a fine brush was used and the modeling carefully built up using thin washes.

Gouache

Gouache colors are superb for painting on a small, intimate scale. They are water-based and come in a wide range of colors. They can be used as a transparent wash or opaquely to dry as flat color. They can also be used in a broader fashion to give a painterly texture. Their beauty lies in their versatility, and this should be exploited to the full, creating in a single painting a variety of surfaces both transparent and opaque.

Any type of paper can be used for gouache, as long as it is stretched or is thick enough not to buckle.

Left: *A middle range of soft brushes is most useful for gouache.*

Below: *Three examples of gouache application: left, glazing; center, impasto; right, free brushwork.*

Choosing paints

Gouache colors are available in two qualities. The cheaper range of colors, usually called poster paints, are sold in pots of varying sizes and can be bought singly or in sets of six, eight, or twelve basic colors.

The more expensive and extensive range are called Designer's Gouache and are available in tubes. The permanence of the color is rated by a star or alphabet system. The brilliance and saturation of the colors is achieved by a heavy and not too finely ground pigment content, combined with a slight lowering of the amount of binding medium.

Colors for the palette

Use a clean, plastic palette, preferably white, so that the small quantities of color can be seen clearly and correctly against it.

Above: *Using the medium in a controlled and precise way, the rich, low-key harmonies of this picture demonstrate the wide possibilities of gouache, its use to convey solid, opaque form and texture together with a delicate, watercolor-like atmosphere.*

Below: *Gouache can also be used in a more vigorous way to convey the mood and atmosphere of a less intimate motif. Opaque areas in the sky are balanced against a wash treatment of the trees and river. The whole painting will dry quickly at its different levels.*

An expressive picture can result from using gouache in a direct way. In stage one the areas are defined and underlying color is applied with a large brush using heavily diluted paint. In stage two a build up of tone and color takes place. The dark area of the buildings and trees are applied as broad masses, over which lighter detailing will take place. The last stage is built up by a confident multiplicity of strokes, with no need for blending.

1

2

3

A suggested range of colors would include the following; red ochre, flame red, alizarin crimson, cadmium yellow, lemon yellow, chromium oxide (green), sap green, cobalt blue, Prussian blue, and white.

There are two types of white in gouache, and they should be selected with the desired effect in mind. Permanent white has a high pigment content and covers well, though it does make colors somewhat chalky. Zinc white has a low pigment content, is more transparent, and is useful when glazing one color over another. A black can be mixed using roughly equal quantities of Indian red and Prussian blue.

Gouache colors tend to crack if applied too thickly, but this can be prevented by using a proprietary acrylizing or plasticizing medium. They also have a tendency to dry slightly darker than when wet in the case of light colors, and slightly lighter in the case of dark ones, though this will not disturb any but the most exacting colorist.

Brushes

A selection of soft brushes will be required, either of sable or the new nylon equivalents. Sable and ox hair mixture brushes can also be used. Brushes consisting of pure ox or squirrel hair tend to be less springy than the sable or nylon, and therefore not quite as easy to control.

Samuel Marshall.

A useful selection of brushes to begin with would include: a ¾-inch flat brush for covering large areas; a size 4 and a size 6 round brush for covering smaller areas and for most of the modeling (the round brushes can be brought to a fine point for quite detailed work); a size 1 brush for the most finely detailed work.

This selection can later be supplemented with a personal choice from the large variety of brushes available. All brushes will repay careful treatment by extended life and greater consistency. Never allow paint to dry on the bristles and do not leave brushes standing in water for long periods. After use, rinse thoroughly, removing excess water and shaping to a point.

Basic painting method

Draw out your composition either in pencil or in a very dilute blue. Flood the first colors on with water in a generous wash to cover the entire composition. From this you can build up the colors more opaquely. If you are covering a large area with one color, mix sufficient color to cover it in one go. Otherwise you will have the problem of matching the color, which can be difficult. Use the brush that is appropriate for the job; do not try to cover large areas with a small brush. Practice applying the paint both opaquely and as a transparent wash until you have mastered the techniques.

Watercolor

Much of today's great watercolor tradition stems from the paintings of the masters of the eighteenth and nineteenth centuries, whose work set a standard of technical virtuosity and artistic sensibility by which all subsequent work in the medium has been measured.

Paints

Watercolor is pure pigment, finely ground from various natural mineral and vegetable substances, bound with glycerine. It is sold in pans or half pans or in two different sizes of tubes. The paint is graded by quality and classified by degree of permanence. Cheaper ranges are available as student quality.

Surfaces

The most usual surface or support for watercolor painting is paper. To obtain the maximum potential from artists' quality watercolors, a rag-based paper should be used.

Paper is manufactured in a wide variety of weights and textures. The heavier the paper, the more expensive it is. A workable range would extend from 90 to 200 pounds. Textures are normally specified in three grades: rough, hot pressed (HP), and cold pressed (CP).

Lighter weight papers should be stretched onto a firm wooden board using packaging tape. A good paper will stand up to a certain amount of rough treatment and hold the color on the surface, giving optimum freshness and brightness. Good-

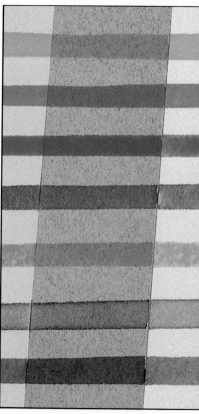

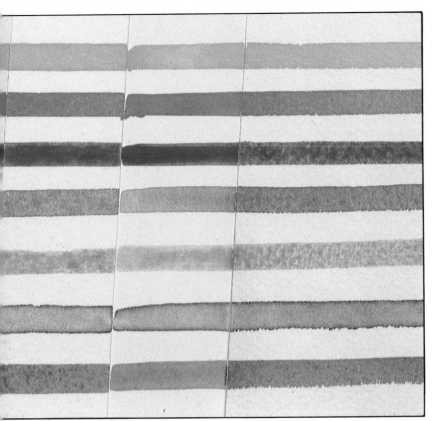

Left: *This chart containing a selection of quality, rag-based papers of different weights and surfaces, demonstrates how color is affected tonally and texturally by the various surfaces. All papers can be readily obtained from art supply shops. Experiment to see which ones suit your requirements best.*

quality paper is gelatine-sized throughout.

The manufacturer's name or mark can be read by holding the paper up to the light. The side from which it can be read correctly is the right side to use.

Brushes

Brushes should be the best quality that you can afford. Sable has the softness, re-silience, and water-holding qualities necessary for the finest control. Nylon brushes are now widely available and are worth trying. Applying broad washes

Opposite: *Good quality brushes are important when using watercolor, sometimes combined with gouache or inks.*

Right: *By covering each of the halves of the head in turn the techniques used to achieve the finished image can be seen. Although the glazes are used very thinly on the right they immediately begin to model the form and place the main features. Further controlled glazes complete the substance and color of the head.*

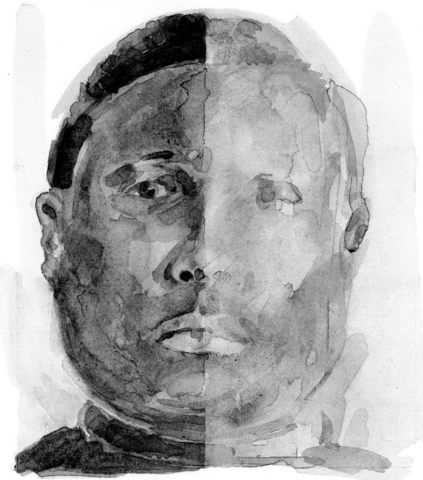

45

calls for a large, pliable brush, shape being of personal preference. Flat, round, or square brushes are available made of sable, ox, or squirrel hair.

Painting techniques

The techniques of applying the paint to the chosen surface call for a personal choice. Nolde, Cotman, De Wint, Cézanne, Segonzac, all masters of watercolors, used techniques of very differing character, ranging from highly organized thin washes built up in glazes to a solid, almost impasto, use of the medium. The small, mosaic-like areas of a Prendergast contrast with the large calm areas of a De Wint.

In watercolor painting the luminosity and purity of the colors are exploited by allowing the natural white of the paper to strike through even the darkest tones. If using a tinted paper, then any whites or luminous areas such as clouds are best conveyed by the use of diluted gouache color. This is a wholly acceptable introduction; Turner and many of his contemporaries had no qualms about using gouache and watercolor together.

Colors appear to be fresher when used on CP or rough paper as the texture of the paper

Right: *Stretching paper for watercolor; tear or cut four strips of ¾-inch packaging tape slightly longer than the sides of the board. Tear or cut paper to size about 1½-inches smaller all around than the board. Read the watermark on the paper to determine which is the right side and mark one corner.*

Submerge the paper in water, being careful not to crease it and thus weaken the fibers. Leave to soak for five to fifteen minutes, depending on the weight of the paper. The heavier the paper, the longer it should be soaked. Lift out

carefully and allow the water to run from one corner until the flow becomes a slow drip. Place the paper squarely on the board, marked side uppermost, and with a dampened hand smooth all air bubbles out to the edges. Dampen packaging tape sparingly – too much water causes it to curl and washes off the gum – and burnish down, half on the paper, half on the board. Gently remove surplus water from the paper with a tissue, giving special attention to areas where packaging tape and paper meet. Leave flat to dry naturally.

A fluid technique displays to good advantage the freshness and directness of watercolors. A combination of wet into wet and overglazing enables broad masses as well as the more detailed parts to be handled quickly and easily. No preliminary underdrawing was done as this would have impaired the spontaneity of the work. The paper used had a hard finish which kept the color on the surface and helped to retain its brilliance.

causes a minute breakdown of the wash, giving a natural sparkle of light and dark tones to the painting.

HP paper is valuable for use with a technique which employs small overlapping areas, strictly controlled, as the means of building up form and atmosphere. Cozens, Cézanne, or Prendergast could be studied as exponents of this technique.

To some degree, the motif you are painting will determine your handling and technique, so be flexible in your approach. A seascape will obviously demand a quicker, broader, and therefore more fluid treatment than a still life.

A watercolor can soon show the effects of sluggish or tentative handling, and overworking is another factor which immediately begins to obscure the paper's great contribution of translucency. Although watercolor can be applied in an impastolike manner, it is worth remembering that the finest work shows fluidity, atmosphere, and spontaneity.

Painting on location

Equipment for watercolor painting should include the following: stretched paper (either on a frame or drawing board) or a good quality watercolor block; a light but sturdy easel and a folding stool; a good range of artists' quality colors with extra pens or tubes of the colors you use most; a selection of brushes; a waterproof satchel and box containing blotting paper, a sharp knife (for scratching out highlights), a small natural sponge, a cloth or rag, cottonwool buds (for lifting out highlights), pencils, an eraser, and one or two mediums if you like them. Oxgall is always useful, but you will soon find what suits you best. Finally, you will need large, stable, plastic containers to hold clean water.

Above: *Direct but carefully considered brush work was used in this still-life of an old boat. The boat's supports have been left uncompleted to show how both light and dark tones may be the starting point for depicting objects. No preliminary drawing was made, but working in the center of the large sheet of paper ensured that the motif would safely fit. A light wash was quickly laid over the white paper before work began, to subdue the glare on a sunny day.*

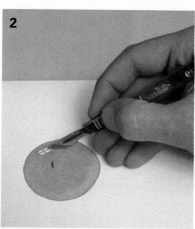

Left: *Watercolor can take many forms and can be altered by technical devices once applied. The photographs show: lifting broad highlights (figure 1); scratching detailed highlights (figure 2); painting slowly and deliberately wet into wet (figure 3); painting quickly wet into wet, giving a diffuse line effect (figure 4).*

Opposite: *Using a limited number of low-key colors, small overlapping areas of color were used to convey the masonry and fragmented tones of the motif. The overall use of warm color has been offset by carefully placed, cool (blue) notes to avoid a monochromatic effect.*

The subject of this step-by-step watercolor was carefully chosen, with the village in the middle distance, and the interesting geometric shapes of the buildings contrasting well with the gentle slopes of the tree-clad valley. The diagonal line of the fence breaks up the foreground.

1.   A carefully considered pencil drawing was made using an HB pencil on a medium weight paper with a soft surface, to indicate the angles of the roofs and walls of the buildings. Some of the main tonal areas were lightly shaded in as an aid to assessing the composition of the motif. The color of the sky was lightly washed in.

2.   In the second stage the pencil drawing was slightly erased, and the shaded areas were completely removed. The tints of the foliage and the pale tones of the buildings and fence were washed in using a size 5 sable brush. The importance of the areas of snow as a strong design factor in the picture became immediately apparent. No further work was done on the sky at this stage.

3. Mid tones were now added to the buildings to convey the solidity of the forms, and to the fence. A darker tone was placed in the windows and doorway to give depth. The sky received additional layers of color. Shadow areas were added across the snow. Some foliage and a build up of the pattern formed by the branches of the trees were indicated. Specific detailing of foliage and stonework, slates, etc. is not added until the overall tones in the painting are correctly balanced. Heavy tones can upset this balance and require correction. This can be time-consuming, particularly in cold weather, as drying times are prolonged in low temperatures.

4. The sky was completed, and when dry, the pattern of fine branches was added, using small brushes. The tones of the branches should be carefully evaluated and indicated, without reworking, as it is not easy to remove a mistake at this stage. The patterns of stonework and slates, the texture of the wooden fence, and the blades of grass in the foregound were the finishing touches.

Mixed media

Mixed media is the use of different paint media together. The water-based paints such as acrylic, gouache, watercolor, and even pencil, crayon, and pastel, can be used effectively in the same painting. The basic rule for using water-based and oil-based media in the same painting is to apply the water-based media first, overlaid by the oil paint, since the water-based paint will not adhere to the oil.

Pastels in particular are ideal to mix with other media, especially watercolor, used either as a base or an overlay. Degas experimented widely with pastel, using it with charcoal and even over a thin application of oil paint and turpentine.

Collage

The sheer weight and diversity of photographic and printed matter now existing has produced a variety of new techniques available for artistic expression.

Collage is probably the most straightforward of these techniques. It consists of using colored materials to create an image or picture. There is no real limitation to the materials used; however, it must be possible for them to be stuck on a support, and for this reason weight is of prime importance. The most useful materials are colored cloths and papers, the latter often being taken from glossy magazines and chosen for their colors and textures.

A similiar process was used to great effect by Matisse in his later years, using paper colored with gouache and subsequently cut to shape. The technique allows a diversity of handling; the paper can be cut or torn,

Opposite below: *A variety of tools and media were used in this portrait. A basic black conté drawing was worked over in watercolor, acrylics and colored ink.*

Right: *Watercolor (left half) and acrylics (right half) have very different covering and textural qualities. In this picture both are applied over black ink.*

Below: *The collage was created by first drawing the composition and using colored paper torn rather than cut from magazines to create the final image. It is a good idea to lay out the pieces of paper in front of you before sticking them down.*

overlapped or separated, to create a vibrant mosaic of color.

As an initial excursion into this field, try rendering a conventional composition such as a still life or portrait using paper cut from magazines instead of paint. Further inspiration can be gained by looking at the work of Kurt Schwitters, who executed interesting compositions using bus and theater tickets of all descriptions.

Montage

Montage provides an interesting alternative use for photographic and printed matter. In this case, however, the material is scanned for its content and imagery, as opposed to its color and texture. The images are cut out and repositioned to create new images and situations which can be attractive, ironic, or bizarre.

Both of these techniques can be used in conjunction with normal painterly practices or on their own. If, however, you intend to use a printed image on paint, you might enjoy the delicacy which can be derived from a technique used by the American artist Robert Rauschenberg. This consists of taking printed material and offsetting it onto the painted support by the use of an oil or spirit which melts the ink. If an oil-based paint has been used, the process may be as simple as placing the printed image face down on the surface and rubbing the back. Otherwise it will be necessary to dampen the image with turpentine or linseed oil before again placing it face down and transferring the image by rubbing the reverse side.

Wax resist

As an alternative to the use of existing material, original work can be built up by the use of the wax-resist method. Greasy material such as candle wax drawn onto the surface of the painting will prevent a water-based paint from adhering. Alternatively, a spirit-based gum may be used. The gum may be subsequently dissolved, enabling this previously covered area to accept paint.

The beauty of this technique is the accidental effects which arise. It is almost impossible to be certain of the results that will be obtained, and the process therefore encourages a certain degree of freedom of execution. Free experimentation is the key to this kind of work.

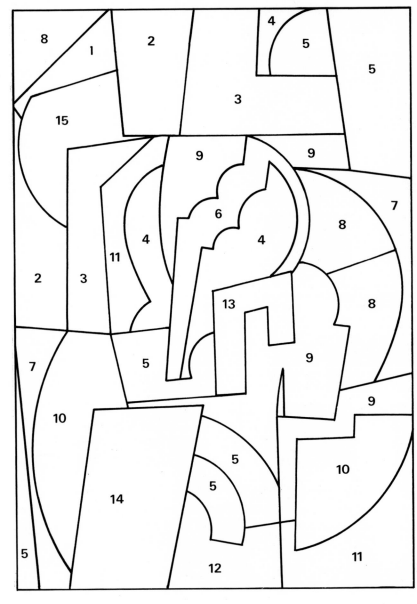

Opposite: *This powerful and colorful abstract painting contains a variety of media and forms a highly sophisticated design in which color, shape and texture both satisfy and intrigue.*

Key:
 1. Pencil burnished on textured surface.
 2. Colored pencil over wax resist.
 3. Ink over oil pastel and graphite.
 4. Colored pencil
 5. Colored ink over colored pencil.
 6. White wax crayon over colored pencil and ink.
 7. Pencil over graphite.
 8. Oil pastel over colored pencil.
 9. Oil pastel and graphite.
10. Wax crayon over oil pastel.
11. Graphite over oil pastel.
12. Colored pencil and graphite.
13. Colored pencil with pastel.
14. White wax crayon over colored pencil.
15. Wax crayon.

Advanced techniques

Everyone who is interested in becoming an artist should try to develop an appreciation of the pictorial qualities apparent in everyday life. Traveling to work can provide the opportunity to educate oneself to observe and note the enormous range of possible subject matter. People, singly or in groups, their different attitudes, ages and dress, the texture of torn posters, the effect of daylight and artificial light on objects and scenes; all are subjects which have been the raw material for masterly paintings.

Visits to art galleries and exhibitions are also very important. Looking at an Edward Hopper painting, for example, one can appreciate the pictorial drama of using dramatic eye-levels, color interpretation and powerful compositional and tonal devices. This awareness helps us to evaluate our own work, and prevents an early development of conventional attitudes. Nearly all great painters have been influenced by the work of preceeding or contemporary artists.

Tone

In visual terms, tone is the darkness or lightness of any color, including black and gray; it is the world as revealed by light and shade. When we draw in line, what we are actually doing is indicating by contour where one volume ends or turns as revealed by light. However, a painting or drawing that is tonally complete is one in which the tonal element predominates.

The remarkable lighting effects for which Rembrandt is remembered are clearly evident in this painting, Self Portrait aged Sixty-three. *Subtle modeling allows light to flow over the face and the hands, while an eloquent simplification is evident in the rest of the figure.*

Looking at a Rembrandt portrait, one can see that the face emerges from a dark background in which nothing is distinctly defined; thus, the face is thrown into sharp contrast, almost evoked from the canvas.

This is achieved by initially laying down a thin wash or glaze of a dark background color and working solid, middle tones of the face into it. The darker tones follow to model the form. At this stage the colors applied will require modification to create a harmonious whole, and this applies to the background colors also. When you are satisfied that all parts of the canvas are working together tonally, the painting can be refined to describe the form more accurately. Finally, the detail and highlights are added.

Tone in abstract

This involves quite an extreme use of tone but, in its normal use, it is the stock in trade of all figurative artists. Abstract painters use it also; the apparent lack of a recognizable image can be deceptive. The abstract painter also deals with form in space and with atmosphere. At the beginning of the abstract movement, artists questioned why painting had to illustrate familiar objects before it was valued. They reasoned that,

In this exercise in manipulating shape and mass, a series of repeat shapes change and increase in size as the idea is developed across the canvas. The exercise is made more interesting if the shapes are allowed to emerge "naturally" from the background, using a dark-colored surface and painting the background first, in lighter colors.

since music is an abstract art which is expressive without being illustrative of the everyday world, the same could be true of painting.

They found a parallel to every aspect of music; like it, painting deals with color, tone, pitch, harmony, discord, point, and counterpoint.

Marc Rothko, the American abstract expressionist painter, dealt with tone in an abstract and atmospheric way. He painted fields of very dark colors onto canvases, often of massive proportions. During the more mature period of his work these paintings became dark, sometimes almost black. On top of the fields he painted atmospheric and diffused rectangles, causing them to float in the dark space of the canvas without any attempt at elaborate composition. The tones of the rectangles he would alter only very slightly from the background tone, thus producing an extraordinary effect of atmospheres suspended and oscillating in space.

Try experimenting yourself with this use of tone, varying the colors but keeping the same tonal value, that is to say, the same grade of lightness or darkness of color.

Painters like Robert Motherwell used dark organic shapes painted with energetic, physical marks. Motherwell's paintings also have what might be called syncopated rhythm, because the bold compositions often set up regular shapes, sometimes almost symmetrical yet slightly off-beat by virtue of the fact that the shapes are altered by chance elements as is often the case in natural organic forms. Attempt to enhance your sense of rhythm by taking a shape and practicing painting it over and over again, examining and modifying it each time in different ways. This exercise is invaluable for increasing your powers of perception.

The archetypal action painter, Jackson Pollock, dealt with rhythm and tone in the most interesting and unexpected ways. He dripped and trailed paint across the surface of his canvases in rhythmic patterns, allowing the threads of paint to interweave across one another, creating a fine mesh of lines. He thereby produced an illusion of a vast complexity of forms.

The impressionistic effects of light and atmosphere are monochromatically conveyed in Monet's Flood at Giverny. *The shapes of the trees provide a necessary rhythm. across the picture.*

Opposite: *Pissarro's painting,* The Côtes des Boeufs at L'Hermitage near Pontoise *combines Impressionist philosophy of light and atmosphere with the traditional norms of form and solidity.*

Above: *This striking composition by Seurat,* Le Bec du Hoc, *shows his interest in the scientific color theories of the day.*

One only has to follow one of the threads of paint across the canvas to appreciate its rhythmic qualities.

Pollock achieved his effects by intuitive positioning of the splashes of color and direction of the dripped trails of paint rather than by a preconcieved sense of order. The paintings are most effective when carried out on a large scale so that the observer is able to stand close to the canvas and, in doing so, is absorbed by the strands of paint meandering across the fields and splashes of color. The observer thereby relives the making of the painting.

An impression of color

The use of color by painters such as Monet, Pissarro, and Sisley is very interesting. The Impressionist philosophy was that, instead of a change of tone, a change of color is equally valid. Many of their paintings, particularly those of Monet, are very brightly colored, almost of a single tone, but with such changes of color that the canvas almost appears to vibrate with pent-up energy. This theory was taken further by the French Post-Impressionists Bonnard and Vuillard, whose beautiful figure paintings are somewhat difficult to decipher at first because of the unexpected use of pattern, tone, and color.

Try taking a painting of your own, or one that you admire by one of the masters and rendering it in a scheme of colors without altering the tones. This will give you a feeling for the difference between tone and color; it is important to be clear about the distinction.

A contemporary of the Impressionists, Georges Seurat, was also interested in color. His paintings, however, were constructed more scientifically than those of the Impressionists. The canvases, which were painted during a period of great scientific advance, mirror in their execution the belief in the validity of science as a modern panacea. Seurat applied paint to the canvas as dots or strokes of pure color. These demonstrated the then new optical theories; the color being mixed optically by the eye of the observer, as opposed to physically by the artist.

The composition of his paintings was also tightly constructed, obeying the classical rules of aesthetics, based upon the perfect rectangle, and a proportion known as the "Golden Section". The completed paintings, for all their theoretical construction and careful execution, have a life of their own. Some of his landscapes, viewed from a distance, shimmer with light.

Another painter often classed with the Impressionists was Paul Cézanne. Though some of his works correspond to the appearance of Impressionist canvases, his intentions and aspirations were far removed from that area. This is demonstrated by the thickness of the

paint on many of the canvases of his middle period, which were heavily worked in an attempt to construct the subject on the canvas.

During Cézanne's mature period, he retained the bright colors of the Impressionist palette, while the application of paint became thinner and more precisely controlled.

A problem central to Cézanne's interests consisted of reconstructing the visible world on the canvas in terms of geometric shapes, namely the cube, the sphere, and the cone. In this, he was the precursor of cubism, and his work was later admired and studied by Braque and Picasso, as a starting point from which they produced their cubist paintings.

This is, however, an oversimplification. While geometric shapes can be seen to be the basis used to build the composition on the canvas, it was the construction which was the important factor to the artist.

Cézanne required of his art solidity and durability. He therefore used the transient nature of light to reveal shape and space in the form of planes which either advance or recede on the picture surface.

In the earliest days of abstract painting, color was the area of major importance for artists such as Wassily Kandinsky. This artist felt that color had a symbolic association and therefore was a universal language. Kandinsky was a member of a school of painting known as the Blue Rider; the title was taken from the subject of one of Kandinsky's earliest canvases in this style. Their use of color was based on a considered, though expressive arrangement, sometimes based on things seen, but often stylized into almost abstract shapes.

A contemporary of Kandinsky, Johann Itten, looked upon color as a seminal subject. He was a theorist who wrote a book in which he discussed the various qualities of color, for example, discordant color, when a color with a normally dark tone is set against a color of a normally light tone. This type of juxtaposition can often be seen in the paintings of artists such as Kandinsky, Paul Klee, and their contemporaries.

Many artists have found a life's work in the exploration of the subtleties of color. Your aim as a painter is to discover in your own work the area of study which interests you most; it might be light or form, color or tone, texture or composition. Any aspect is worthy of study, and, when you have chosen an area, or it has chosen you, see how other artists have used it and where it occurs in nature and your environment and develop it as far as you can. Above all else, be prepared to look at everything with a clear and discerning eye.

Opposite: *In this portrait,* The Gardener, *Cézanne's grasp of color harmonies is seen to good advantage. The background colors which start with cool blues on the left gradually wrap around and almost envelop the gardener in green organic forms. Little distinction is made between background colors and those used to depict the figure, which closely associates the gardener with his surroundings.*

Right: *This abstract shows interesting juxtapositions and changes of tone and color.*

Framing

The keynote of framing any artwork successfully is simplicity. In most cases drawings, watercolors, and pastels should be framed under glass for protection.

Mounting the picture

To separate the surface of the work and the glass, a card mount is necessary. Determine the width of mount that looks best by laying strips of paper of different widths around the work, leaving a slightly wider margin on the bottom edge (figure 1).

Measure the size of the picture defined by the strips, and cut a window out of a generous-sized piece of card, and bevel the edges (figure 2).

Hold the knife at the angle indicated in the drawing and draw the craft knife the full length of the cut in one movement, taking care not to overcut onto the corners. Always use the sharpest blade possible and a properly designed straight edge of hardened stainless steel with a beveled edge.

Attach the original artwork to a heavy backing board using a soluble gum or gummed paper hinges along the top edge only and flap the mount over the original as shown (figure 3).

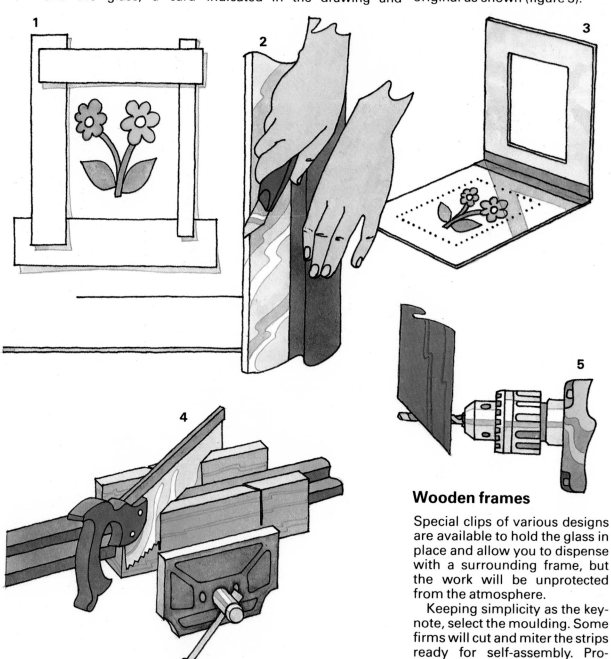

Wooden frames

Special clips of various designs are available to hold the glass in place and allow you to dispense with a surrounding frame, but the work will be unprotected from the atmosphere.

Keeping simplicity as the keynote, select the moulding. Some firms will cut and miter the strips ready for self-assembly. Professional framers use precision steel miter blocks which have the saw clamped in place to ensure the correct angle is cut. This equipment is expensive but worth having if you intend doing all your own framing.

Miters can be cut using a wooden miter block, if you take care and use a very sharp tenon saw. Cut the molding into lengths approximating to each side of the picture and overcut a few inches on each length, to allow for the square of the molding from which to cut the 45 degree miter. A canvas size 20 x 30 inches, using a 3-inch wide molding will require minimum lengths of 26 and 36 inches for each side. Secure the miter block to the work bench with clamps, or use a vice. (When using a vice protect the molding with some kind of padding). If possible, clamp the molding to be cut in the secured miter block. Make all your right-hand cuts at the same time (figure 4).

Drill holes through the miters slightly smaller in diameter than the nails to be used (figure 5). Join a long and short side together, after applying proprietary wood glue to the surfaces to be joined. Tap the nails

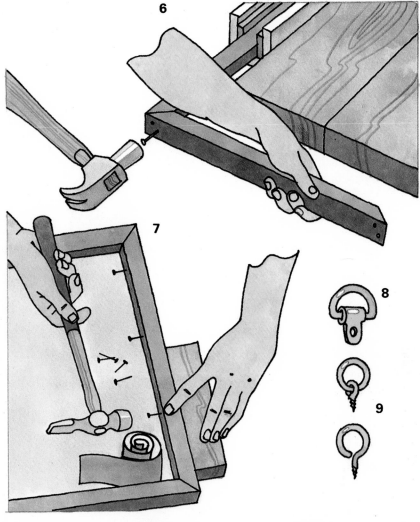

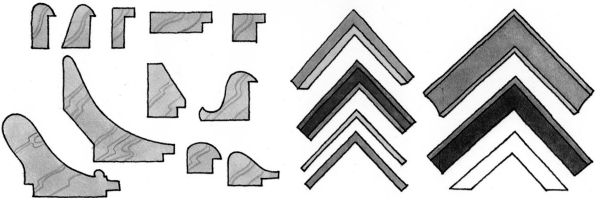

in gently and leave to dry (figure 6). Join the two glued and pinned sections together, supporting the diagonally opposite corners to prevent stress.

Assembling the picture

Buy or cut special picture glass to size, slightly smaller than the overall frame, and make sure that the glass is absolutely free from dirt and fingerprints. Instead of picture glass, which is quite expensive, you can use ordinary window glass.

Put the frame face down; place glass, mount, and artwork and backing board in position in the frame. Tap in light backing pins or wire brads at 6-inch intervals (figure 7), bracing the frame with a piece of wood as each is inserted. Seal the back with 2-inch packaging or similar tape. "D" rings (figure 8) should be inserted in the backing board before assembly, or screw eyes (figure 9) can be inserted in the frame for hanging.

Appreciation

An appreciation of the range of materials available, and the techniques which the artist can use, will help you to recognize the qualities of many paintings – not simply "works of art".

Moreover, your enjoyment of painting will increase with your developing knowledge. Keep up with the latest ideas in art and develop an interest in your local art collection. New techniques are constantly being discovered and modified. If you can, join your local art classes and do not hesitate to ask for professional advice. Sharing and trying new techniques is an essential part of the growth of any artist.

Above: *The interlocking rhythms and dynamic brushwork of this Provencal landscape,* Cornfield with Cypress Trees, *by Van Gogh comes from his mature period. Colors are placed directly and unerringly. Traditional color theory is very evident in the use of cool purples to convey the distant hills and the warm colors of the corn in the foreground of the picture which was probably painted in one session.*

Left: *Monet's paintings of the daily world of entertainment and café life like this one,* The Waitress, *were also a favorite theme of the new generation of French painters which included Degas, Lautrec and Renoir. Monet painted his forms in flat areas of color, modeling further and correcting by working wet into wet. Although associated with the Impressionist movement, Monet was also particularly influenced by the work of Francisco Goya.*